He Is ...

A STUDENT'S GUIDE TO KNOWING GOD

Carrie D. Rogers

ISBN: 9781092295413

To Haley, Rylie, Coleman,
Mason, Ashley,
and all my "pseudo-children."
(You know who you are!)
May you come to know, trust,
and boldly proclaim HE IS!

TABLE OF CONTENTS

A NOTE TO YOU

Welcome to *He Is ... A Student's Guide to Knowing God*.

I want you to know right from the start that the purpose of this study isn't simply about seeking more knowledge. Stuffing our heads with information about God isn't our end goal. Our end goal is more trust. We want to know God more so that we can trust Him more.

DO YOU WANT TO TRUST GOD MORE?

If you do, you've opened the right book. So what does knowing God have to do with trusting God? Listen to how David puts it in Psalm 9:

> Those who know your name trust in you, for you, O LORD, do not abandon those who search for you. (Psalm 9:10)

This verse teaches us that there is something special, something powerful even, about knowing God's name.

Anytime we come across the concept of God's name in Scripture, the authors are referring to who God is and how He works in our lives (His character and nature).

GOD'S NAME = HIS CHARACTER

This verse, then, explains that those who know and experience the character of God (those who know who He is) will grow in their trust of Him. In fact, His name actually inspires trust.

Let me explain it another way.

How often do you inspect a chair before you sit in it? Not very often, right? Most of the time, you and I don't think twice before

1

we sit in a chair because we're well acquainted with chairs. We know what a chair is and we know how it works, so we trust it will hold us up.

The same is true with God. If you and I want to trust God more, we first need to understand who He is and how He works in our lives. We need to know that when we put the full weight of our faith on Him, He has the ability to hold us up.

That's our goal. More trust.

Every week of this book's reading, you will be introduced to a new name of God and, with that name, three character traits or qualities of God that will help us to know and trust Him more.

But before we begin, there are two big things I'm asking from you:

1: COMMIT TO THE STUDY

Will you commit to really do this study with me? Read the pages, answer the questions, and look up the verses. You are welcome to write all over this book. Jot down notes as you read, underline, star — these pages are yours!

2: SEEK GOD PERSONALLY

The purpose of this book is to know and trust God more, so as you read and learn, I challenge you to really seek God personally. God says that when we seek Him, we will find Him, and in the finding, we will never be the same (Jeremiah 29:13–14a).

Are you with me?

Unless noted, all Bible references are from the New Living Translation (NLT). All definitions are from dictionary.com.

WEEK ONE

GOD

#1 He is ...

OUR SOURCE

(God: Elohim)

In the beginning God created the heavens and the earth.
(Genesis 1:1)

The first recorded name of God is found in the first sentence of the first chapter of the first book of the Bible. You actually just read it in the verse above. Did you catch it? Usually when we come across the name *God* in the Bible, we don't think much about it. But in the Hebrew language, which is the original language of the Old Testament, this name is loaded with important truths that can help us know God more.

The word *God* in Hebrew is the name *Elohim,* which means "mighty or strong." In the context of this verse, we can learn several important truths about God. We'll look at the first today.

"In the beginning God ..." From these first four words in the Book of Genesis, we are challenged to wrap our limited minds around some enormous truth. In the beginning, before the world began and time existed — before the sun, the moon, the stars — there was only God. God is the Source, or starting place, of all things.

The dictionary defines *source* as "a person, place, or thing from which something comes." So, when we refer to God as the Source, we are saying that everything that exists begins or comes from Him.

God is the Source of every life, every blessing, every provision, and every purpose of our lives. The more we grow in our relationship with God, the more we'll see that everything we need flows from our relationship with Him.

Hang in there with me ... we've only just begun.

<< ASK >>

Have you ever thought about when and where all of life began? (Circle one) Yes or No

If everything comes from God, how great and impressive must He be?

Have you ever thought about drawing your strength and energy from God as your Source? How could recognizing God as your Source impact your daily life?

<< PRAY >>

Father, thank You for revealing Yourself as *God,* the Source of all existence. Teach me how to bring all my needs to You each day, trusting that everything I need will flow out of my relationship with You.

<< LIVE >>

On the next page, make a list of your needs today. For example, do you need patience with a younger sibling, strength to get through a hard season, healing from a sports injury, or help controlling your tongue when someone is rude to you?

Today's needs:

Will you trust God to be the Source of everything you listed above? Talk to Him about your needs today. He is able!

#2 He is ...
CREATOR

(God: Elohim)

He is the God who made the world and everything in it.
(Acts 17:24a)

The story of the Bible begins with these ground-breaking words: "In the beginning God created the heavens and the earth." Genesis 1 paints the picture of creation in big strokes and stunning colors as our strong and mighty Creator God spoke the earth into existence. With the words "Let there be ..." waters separated, the sun blazed, seeds sprouted, and a whale took its first dive in the deep blue sea. Then, after six days of creating — with the creation of man and woman as both the highlight and grand finale — God looked upon His works and labeled them "very good" (Genesis 1:31).

Have you looked around lately? Our Creator makes *good* things. Two times a day He paints the sky with amazing color just to wow us at the start and close of each day. He made birds to sing, lions to roar, and dogs to curl up in our laps. Our Creator God stacked together rocks to form mountains, He scattered stars to create pictures across the dark night sky, and He knit you together in your mother's womb (Psalm 139:13).

Yes, YOU are part of God's amazing creation.

In the New Testament, the apostle Paul expounds further by saying that we are God's masterpiece, created on purpose and with a purpose (Ephesians 2:10). Is that how you view yourself — as one of God's creative masterpieces?

Whether we believe it or not, the truth is you and I are some of God's very best work. God didn't do an amazing job on all of creation, then mess up when He got to us. Our Creator doesn't make mistakes.

God created you just the way you are — from the color of your eyes to the shape of your little pinky toes — on purpose and with a purpose. And when He steps back to look at His creation, He smiles and calls you "very good."

<< ASK >>

What are some of your favorite things that God created?

When you look in the mirror, do you usually spend more time appreciating the unique creation that you are or pointing out and picking apart all your flaws? Why?

List at least five great things about the way God made you. (Don't worry! This isn't bragging. I want you to practice recognizing and appreciating God's good work in you!)

1.

2.

3.

4.

5.

<< PRAY >>

Father God, thank You for revealing Yourself to me as God, the Creator of the whole earth and everything in it. Help me to accept the truth today that I am Your masterpiece, created on purpose and with a purpose.

<< LIVE >>

Write the following verse on a notecard and put it by your bathroom mirror. Or, better yet, grab an erasable marker and write the verse directly on your mirror for some "in your face" truth!

> I praise you because I am fearfully and wonderfully made; your works are wonderful, I know that full well. (Psalm 139:14 NIV)

Read this verse aloud every time you look in the mirror until you believe it's true.

#3 He is …

OUR SUSTAINER

(God: Elohim)

The Son radiates God's own glory and expresses the very character of God, and he sustains everything by the mighty power of his command. (Hebrews 1:3a)

Have you ever been so stressed that you wondered how you were going to keep it all together? Between school, work, chores, sports, and all your other extracurricular activities, it's hard to hold it all together … not to mention you'd also like to have some resemblance of a social life. I get it. Life is hard. But I have some good news for you!

Not only is God the Source and Creator of all things, but He also has the power to hold it all together, every tiny, little detail.

The writer of Hebrews teaches us that Jesus *sustains* everything by the power of His word. The truth of that is stunning to me — it means that the very universe is *upheld, maintained, guided, propelled,* and *held together* simply because Jesus says so. That's big! Yet it's not only the greatness of what He upholds that gets to me. It's the fact that included in that "everything" are you and me.

> Even to your old age and gray hairs
> I am he, I am he who will sustain you.
> I have made you and I will carry you;
> I will sustain you and I will rescue you.
> (Isaiah 46:4 NIV)

Because of Jesus, you and I are held together. We are *carried, supported, maintained,* and *sustained* by the power of our mighty God. You and I don't have to try to hold it all together, which is fabulous because we can't. We were not created to hold everything together on our own.

However, when we choose to look to and trust in Jesus, He does the heavy lifting for us. Jesus sustains *all things*. He holds together our strength, our energy, and our sanity until we fall asleep; our friendships, our mind, and our up-and-down emotions; our schedule, our future, and our every last nerve.

Any time you're feeling overloaded and don't know what to do, imagine God whispering these words to you: "My child, I made you; I am certainly capable of sustaining you. The only question is: Do you trust Me?"

<< ASK >>

What do you usually do when you're feeling overwhelmed and stressed?

How could looking to Jesus as your Sustainer alleviate that stress?

<< PRAY >>

Father God, I praise You for being not only my Source and Creator, but also my Sustainer. When I'm feeling stressed or overwhelmed, remind me that You are the only One who can hold all things together, and help me to trust You to hold it all together for me.

<< LIVE >>

Let's do a brain dump. Below, make a list of everything you feel like you're holding right now. When you're done, write a prayer to God about your list and tell Him that you trust Him (or want to learn to trust Him) to hold all things together for you.

Brain Dump List:

Prayer:

He is ...
OUR SOURCE,
CREATOR,
& SUSTAINER.

Look back over Lessons 1–3. What stuck out to you? Did you learn something new? What is one truth you want to remember about God this week?

<< READ IT >>

- ☐ Psalm 139
- ☐ Isaiah 40:21–31
- ☐ Colossians 1:15–19

<< WRITE IT >>

Look up Revelation 4:11. Write the verse in the space provided.

<< SHARE IT >>

Share with someone the one big truth you learned about God this week. Who are you going to tell? _____
(Now go do it!)

WEEK TWO

LORD

&

THE GOD WHO SEES

#4 He is ...

OUR OWNER

(Lord: Adonai)

The earth is the LORD's, and everything in it. The world and all its people belong to him. (Psalm 24:1)

Have you ever thought about why we call God *Lord*? Maybe you've heard this name spoken in church or from friends long enough that you've started using it too. Whether we know it or not, when we call God our Lord, or *Adonai* in Hebrew, we are declaring two important truths about our relationship with Him. We'll look at the first today.

The first thing we need to understand is that to call God *Lord* is to declare Him Owner of all. The key verse above says that the same God who made the world and everything in it is also the Owner of all. Everything God created belongs to Him. This makes sense, right? After all, if God made all things, certainly He gets to claim the rights of ownership to all things, too. But what about when we're talking about us — human beings created by God?

> Acknowledge that the LORD is God! He made us, and we are his. We are his people, the sheep of his pasture. (Psalm 100:3)

We'll get to the sheep part in a couple of weeks, but for now let's focus on this truth: As believers, you and I fall into the category of God's possession. We are His; we *belong* to the Lord. This truth has the potential to change everything about how we view ourselves and where we fit in this big, wild world, if we let it.

Every one of us has the need to belong — to fit in somewhere and matter to someone. I'll never forget the first day I received my middle school athletics uniform. As cheesy as it sounds, I couldn't wait to get home so I could proudly wear my new school colors for the very first time. You've probably felt that joy and pride of belonging, too.

However, no matter what roles you take on in this life, what teams you make (or don't make), or what the "popular group" thinks of you, God proudly claims you as His very own. The fact that you belong to the Creator of the universe gives you worth, purpose, and order for your life. You are *His*.

Anytime you feel unloved, unimportant, undervalued, or insecure, remember whom you belong to! You *belong* to the Lord.

<< ASK >>

When have you experienced the joy of belonging?

Do you feel like you belong to God? Why or why not?

<< PRAY >>

Heavenly Father, I thank You today for the truth that I belong to You. Anytime I'm feeling unloved, unimportant, undervalued, or insecure, please remind me that You, the Owner of the whole world and everything in it, claim me as Your very own.

<< LIVE >>

Think about your most prized possession. How do you treat/take care of the things you consider most valuable?

As the Lord's most prized possession, you can trust that He both proudly claims you *and* perfectly takes care of you. Now go live with confidence today, remembering that you belong to the Lord.

#5 He is ...

IN CHARGE

(Lord: Adonai)

I said to the LORD, "You are my Master! Every good thing I have comes from you." (Psalm 16:2)

In our last lesson, we learned that when we call God our *Lord,* we are declaring two important truths about our relationship with Him. The first is that He is our Owner; we belong to the Lord.

The second truth we need to understand is that to call God *Lord* is to acknowledge Him as the Master of all (or the One in charge).

Unfortunately, most of us have a pretty messed-up picture of a master/slave relationship because of what we've seen or heard about throughout history regarding the abuse of slaves. This picture in no way resembles our relationship with God as *Lord.* As a matter of fact, the Bible paints a very different picture.

In the Old Testament, the relationship between master and slave was more often one of love and respect. A slave actually had more privileges than the hired help. He was looked at as a member of the family, with the promise that all of his needs for provision would be met by his master. But more than that, the servant was also assured that the master would give him all the help and resources he needed to carry out and accomplish his tasks as servant. The servant could call upon his master for help, whatever the need.

When we call God *Lord,* we are saying that we choose to submit to Him as the One in charge. He's the boss! The opposite is also true. When we refuse to obey God, we're saying that He's really not our Lord. Listen to how Jesus puts it:

"So why do you keep calling me 'Lord, Lord!' when you don't do what I say?" (Luke 6:46)

We can't call Jesus *Lord* in one breath but tell Him that we won't obey in the next. Either He is our Lord (the One whom we obey), or He's not.

As Master, the Lord is not a cruel, demanding, hard-hearted bully. Instead, He is a loving, generous, protective Master who takes you by the hand and walks through life with you. Every good thing you have in this life comes from His mighty hands. Will you surrender your heart to Him today?

<< ASK >>

We all like to feel like we're in charge sometimes, but the reality is, we're not. Who is hardest for you to submit to and obey? Why? (For example, your parents, teachers, boss, or someone else?)

How can seeing God as a loving, generous, protective Master encourage you to trust Him more?

<< PRAY >>

Father God, I understand now that when I call You *Lord,* I am placing myself in Your hands as my Owner and Master. Help me to see my obedience to You as a privilege instead of a duty. I want to grow in my relationship with You.

« LIVE »

If you're ready and willing, get on your knees and talk to God about your desire to know and obey Him as your good and generous Master. If you're not ready to surrender your life to the Lord yet, it's okay. We don't have to pretend to be somewhere we're not. Just be honest with God, and ask Him to grow in your heart the desire to know and trust Him more.

#6 He is ...
PAYING ATTENTION

(The God Who Sees: El Roi)

The LORD is watching everywhere, keeping his eye on both the evil and the good. (Proverbs 15:3)

Have you ever felt invisible? The reality is that sometimes we can be in a huge crowd of people and still feel like no one even notices we're there. If this has ever been true for you, you're not alone. We all wonder sometimes if anyone sees us or if we really matter in this big, wide world. I think that's exactly why God chose to reveal Himself as *El Roi,* the God Who Sees.

The Bible teaches us that no matter where we are or what we're doing, God is paying attention. He sees us, not because He wants to keep track of our rights and wrongs but because He loves us. (Do you realize that God can't take His eyes off you?!?)

This makes me think of the hours I spent with my kids every summer at the pool. Over and over they would yell for me, "Mom! Watch this!" After about the hundredth time, I would tell them, "You don't have to keep asking me to watch you. I see you! I'm watching."

You and I don't have to ask God to watch us. We can trust that He's always paying attention.

> Nothing in all creation is hidden from God. Everything is naked and exposed before his eyes ... (Hebrews 4:13a)

Not only are we not invisible to God, but nothing in all of creation is hidden from His sight. God sees it all — even when we think no one's watching, even when we feel unnoticed, even when we think we're hiding.

God didn't write out the story of your life, then walk away and hope everything turns out for the best. Instead, because of His great love for you, our God is actively watching, paying attention, and personally aware of your every motive and move. He actually knows you better than you know yourself. He's caught every tear you've ever cried, heard every word you've left unspoken, and taken note of every pain and heartache you've suffered. You can rest today knowing that the God of the universe is paying attention. He sees (knows and loves) you.

<< ASK >>

When do you most often feel invisible?

How can you remind yourself that God is always paying attention and will always be there for you in those "invisible" moments?

<< PRAY >>

Heavenly Father, I praise You today for being the God Who Sees. I'm so grateful to know that because of Your great love for me, I can trust that You're always paying attention. Even if I feel like no one else sees or knows me for who I really am, I can trust today (and always) that You know me, You see me, and You will never abandon me.

<< LIVE >>

Every time you look in the mirror today, ask God to give you eyes to see yourself as He does. You are one of His very favorites!

He is ...

OUR OWNER, IN CHARGE, & PAYING ATTENTION.

Look back over Lessons 4–6. What stuck out to you? Did you learn something new? What is one truth you want to remember about God this week?

<< READ IT >>

☐ Isaiah 41:8–10
☐ 1 Peter 2:9–10

<< WRITE IT >>

Look up Psalm 16:2. Write the verse in the space provided.

<< SHARE IT >>

Share with someone the one big truth you learned about God this week. Who are you going to tell? _____
(Now go do it!)

WEEK THREE

LORD

#7 He is ...
CONSTANT

(LORD; Jehovah: Yahweh)

"I am the LORD, and I do not change ..." (Malachi 3:6a)

The most common name for God in the Old Testament is LORD (in all caps). This name is different from the name Lord (in lowercase letters) that we discussed in Lessons #4 and #5. LORD is the Hebrew name *Yahweh,* which is translated as *Jehovah,* or the Great I Am. We'll spend the next three days discovering the character of God as LORD.

You've probably realized by now that everything around us is constantly changing, from trends to technology to your latest crush. In a world where it seems like nothing stays the same, it's important to know that the LORD is constant and unchanging.

> Jesus Christ is the same yesterday, today, and forever. (Hebrews 13:8)

God never changes. From His character and nature to His purposes and promises — everything about God remains the same. His wisdom and power will never increase or diminish. He will never change His mind about His great love for you, and His promise to be with you always is guaranteed. Even though the opinions and values of the world will continue to change with time, God's values and His standard for right living will always remain the same.

The truth of God's constant and unchanging nature is fundamental to His faithfulness. The LORD isn't moody or fickle; He is constant — dependable to the core. That's why He's so often referred to as our Rock. God provides stability and security in a world where nothing stays the same for long.

Next time you feel your world shifting, whether from a natural change (like a new school year) or the ones that take you by surprise (like a big breakup, your parents announcing their divorce, or a big family move), call out to the LORD, our unchanging, immovable God. He will be a safe place for you.

> From the ends of the earth, I cry to you for help when my heart is overwhelmed. Lead me to the towering rock of safety, for you are my safe refuge, a fortress where my enemies cannot reach me. (Psalm 61:2–3)

<< ASK >>

What feelings arise when you're confronted (or presented) with a big change in your life?

What does that mean to you that God is your Rock?

<< PRAY >>

Father God, I'm so grateful to know that You are unchanging. You are constant and dependable in who You are and all You do. Help me to learn to lean on You as my stable Rock in a world that's always changing. Let Your truth be the solid ground under my feet so I won't be shaken. I want to learn to trust in You.

<< LIVE >>

Write down three things about God that you know to be good
and true. (If you can't think of three, ask someone to help you!)

1.

2.

3.

These things about God will never change. Whether you're
making good choices and life seems to be going great, or you're
struggling and life seems to be falling apart, God will always
remain the same. Look to the LORD — He will always be there
for you!

#8 He is ...
PRESENT & ACTIVE

(LORD; Jehovah: Yahweh)

God is our refuge and strength, an ever-present help in trouble.
(Psalm 46:1 NIV)

Do you ever struggle with loneliness? I know it might be hard to admit out loud, but I will let you in on a little secret: Everyone deals with feeling lonely from time to time. Most people don't talk about it because they're afraid that admitting their loneliness makes them sound desperate or friendless. But the reality is that you and I can be surrounded by friends and people who love us, but we can still feel lonely.

When God revealed Himself as LORD way back in Genesis 2, He was introducing Himself as our present and active God. God isn't some far-off cosmic superhero, too preoccupied with flinging stars across the sky and keeping the earth in orbit to notice the last tear you cried or deep sigh you made. He is always with you, actively working in your life in a million ways, both big and small.

One of my favorite verses in the Bible is this one:

> Do not be afraid or discouraged, for the LORD will personally go ahead of you. He will be with you; he will neither fail you nor abandon you. (Deuteronomy 31:8)

I need to remind myself often that the LORD is always with me; I am never alone. And neither are you.

No matter where you go in this life, God has already gone ahead of you, and His Spirit is always with you. Even though your feelings, the world, or even your circumstances might try to convince you otherwise, you are never truly alone. You have the God of the universe with you — He has gone before you, He follows closely behind you, and He will walk beside you every step of the way.

<< ASK >>

Can you think of the last time you felt lonely? When was it?

Does it comfort you or make you nervous to know that God is always with you? Why?

<< PRAY >>

Heavenly Father, I praise You today for being my present and active God. Remind me when I'm feeling lonely that I'm not alone because You are always with me. Thank You for being present and active in my life, especially when I don't realize or forget that You're there.

<< LIVE >>

Sometimes it helps to have something tangible to remind you of God's presence. This week, draw a heart or star (or even the letter "G" for God) on your hand in marker to remind yourself throughout the day that the LORD is present and active with you in every second of your every day. When we start paying attention to our present and active God, we will start seeing Him at work all around us.

#9 He is ...
A PROMISE KEEPER

(LORD; Jehovah: Yahweh)

The LORD always keeps his promises; he is gracious in all he does. (Psalm 145:13b)

Do you remember the first time someone broke a promise to you? Maybe when you were little, a friend looked you straight in the eyes (convincing you of their trust) and made you a promise, but secretly they had their fingers crossed behind their back. Or maybe the promise was made by a sibling, a parent, or extended family member.

We all know what it feels like to have a promise broken. At first, we may feel hurt or disappointment, but over time those unfulfilled promises and broken commitments can grow into a serious lack of trust. It's hard to know whom we can depend on, isn't it?

While we live on this earth, people will continue to fail us. They'll promise us the world and deliver disappointment. You and I will do our share of failing people, too. But it's important to realize that there *is* One we can always depend on — there *is* One whose promises will always be true.

> God is not a man, so he does not lie. He is not human, so he does not change his mind. Has he ever spoken and failed to act? Has he ever promised and not carried it through? (Numbers 23:19)

When God revealed Himself as the LORD, He showed Himself to be the ultimate promise keeper. From this verse (and many others like it), we can learn three important truths:

33

1. God cannot lie. The LORD is incapable of speaking anything less than perfect truth. (And He's never secretly crossing His fingers behind His back either.)

2. God is trustworthy. If God says He will do something, He also has the ability to carry it out. He is not only dependable, but He's also capable. There is nothing God cannot do.

3. God is faithful. God will always follow through on His promises. Although His timing and His ways might be different from ours, we can trust that He will always do what He says He will do.

You can trust today (and always) that God is the greatest promise keeper you will ever know.

<< ASK >>

How do you feel when someone breaks a promise to you?

How do you feel when you break your promise to someone?

How does knowing that God *always* keeps His promises help you to trust Him more?

<< PRAY >>

Father God, I thank You today for always keeping Your promises and loving me no matter what. Grow my faith and help me learn to trust more in Your faithfulness. You are dependable, capable, and trustworthy in all You say and do.

<< LIVE >>

The Bible is full of the promises of God. Read Isaiah 55:10–11. What do these verses tell you about God's faithfulness?

He is ...

CONSTANT, PRESENT & ACTIVE, & A PROMISE KEEPER.

Look back over Lessons 7–9. What stuck out to you? Did you learn something new? What is one truth you want to remember about God this week?

<< READ IT >>

☐ Psalm 102:25–27
☐ Psalm 139:7–10
☐ 2 Timothy 2:13

<< WRITE IT >>

Look up Psalm 105:4. Write the verse in the space provided.

<< SHARE IT >>

Share with someone the one big truth you learned about God this week. Who are you going to tell? _____
(Now go do it!)

WEEK FOUR

GOD MOST HIGH

#10 He is ...
IN CONTROL

(God Most High: El Elyon)

For the LORD *Most High is awesome. He is the great King of all the earth. ... God reigns above the nations, sitting on his holy throne.* (Psalm 47:2, 8)

Do you ever wonder where God is when bad things happen? When you hear news of wars and school shootings and the millions of starving children around the world, do you ever stop to wonder who's really in control? Questions like these are normal, and their answer is found in another one of God's many names.

Because God made everything (God: Elohim) and He owns everything (Lord: Adonai), then He has the right to rule over everything, too. When the Old Testament writers refer to God by the name God Most High (or *El Elyon* in Hebrew), they are referring to God as the King of all kings. He is the strongest of strong — the sovereign ruler over all of creation.

Sovereignty is one of those words that church people often throw around easily, but it's a difficult concept for us to wrap our minds around. God's sovereignty is the way we define God's supreme power and authority — His right to rule. No matter what is going on in this crazy, mixed-up world, God is in control. He is still on His throne.

Saying that God is in control is very different from saying He is controlling. God Most High does not control His creation. He doesn't move us around like puppets on a string. He will never force us to love Him back or make us live our lives according to His ways. But as sovereign ruler, He does have everything under control. After all, God "rules over all, works through all, and is present in all" (Ephesians 4:6 MSG). There is nothing spinning outside of or apart from His supreme reach or rule.

Knowing that God Most High is in control can give us peace of mind when the circumstances of life flip our world upside down. Jesus comforts us with this truth in John 16:

> "I have told you all this so that you may have peace in me. Here on earth you will have many trials and sorrows. But take heart, because I have overcome the world." (John 16:33)

Although troubles in this life are sure to come, Jesus, our conquering King, has overcome the powers of darkness, and He is in control.

There has never been nor will there ever be a time in your life when God drops the ball or turns a blind eye to the circumstances or details of your life. When bad things happen (and especially when you don't understand "why"), you can rest assured that God will work all things out for His glory and your ultimate good (Romans 8:28). God's Word guaranteed!

<< ASK >>

When are the times when you most wonder where God is and if He's really in control?

What are some ways we can properly respond to God as our Ruler and conquering King?

<< PRAY >>

Father God, I praise You today for being God Most High, our sovereign God who is in control. Even though I might not always understand Your ways, teach me how to trust that nothing can happen in my life that is outside of Your sovereign rule.

<< LIVE >>

Will you let go and let God take control of your life today? Remember, God won't force you to submit to Him, but He does want you to know that you can trust Him because He's got everything under control. The choice to believe is up to you!

#11 He is ...
ALL-POWERFUL

(God Most High: El Elyon)

O Sovereign LORD! You made the heavens and earth by your strong hand and powerful arm. Nothing is too hard for you! (Jeremiah 32:17)

When my kids were little, my mom taught them this simple song (with hand motions, of course) about our great, big God. The words of the chorus are playing in my head right now as I think about God Most High, our all-powerful God: "My God is so big, so strong, and so mighty. There's nothing my God cannot do."

God is the only being in heaven or on earth who is omnipotent, which means "all-powerful." His power and might know no end. The concept of God's all-encompassing power is found throughout the Bible, starting with creation in the Book of Genesis and ending with Revelation, the last book of the Bible, when God defeats the devil and reigns for eternity.

Although God's power and might are greater than we can think or imagine, here are three important truths to remember:

1. God can do whatever He wants (Psalm 115:3). God isn't limited to time or space like we are, so He can do whatever He wants whenever He wants. The only thing God can't do is act in ways that are contrary to His perfect, holy nature (like He cannot lie or sin).

2. No one can stop God (Job 42:2). There is no force, no power, and no being equal to God. Although the devil is very real and very powerful, he has no power to restrain, overthrow, withstand, or defeat God Most High.

43

3. Nothing is impossible for God (Mark 10:27). There is *nothing* that God cannot do. Not even death can hold Him down.

Isn't it comforting to know that the God who holds the whole world in His hands holds all His children (including you and me) in His hands, too? There is nothing that can come into our lives — no trial, no temptation, no struggle, no circumstance — that is too big or too hard for our God.

<< A∫K >>

When you think about God's power, what is the first thing that comes to your mind?

What is the benefit of knowing that you can turn to God, with whom nothing is impossible, for help?

How could the knowledge of God's omnipotence affect the way you pray?

<< PRAY >>

Heavenly Father, I praise You today for being our all-powerful God. Remind me when I'm tempted to doubt or fear that I can fully depend on You because even the impossible is possible with You!

<< LIVE >>

Read Ephesians 3:20–21. As followers of Jesus, whose power is at work within us?

Walk with confidence today, knowing that you have the unstoppable, unending, unimaginable power of God Most High at work within you. With God, all things are possible.

#12 He is …

GOOD

(God Most High: El Elyon)

You are good and do only good; teach me your decrees.
(Psalm 119:68)

How do you feel when you get blamed for something you didn't do? If you were to ask my middle child, she would tell you it's the worst! Apparently as the middle child, she gets blamed for far more trouble than she deserves. Maybe you can relate. I bet God can relate, too.

Imagine the countless number of fingers that regularly point to God when bad things happen — when there's a tragedy, when we're inconvenienced, or simply when life doesn't turn out exactly how we wanted. How often do we affirm that God Most High is in control and all-powerful, yet forget that He is also good?

From cover to cover, the Bible consistently affirms and confirms the goodness of God. Everything about God is perfect (He's *way better* than good), and out of the abundance of His goodness flows only that which is good. He's incapable of anything less. Remember, God cannot change. He can't extend an extra measure of goodness to His favorites, then withhold good from the rest of us.

So, why do you think we forget (or worse, distrust) the goodness of God? For most of us, I think it comes down to our perspective. Imagine your perspective as a camera lens — it's the way you view your life, God, and everything else.

When we attempt to define God by looking through the lens of our ever-changing circumstances, God comes out looking broken, distorted, and less than good. However, when we learn to fix our eyes on the immovable character of our good and faithful God, our circumstances begin to take their proper shape. Over time, God opens our eyes to see His goodness everywhere — even (and maybe especially) in the things we label "hard" or "bad."

Listen, friends: Life is hard, the world is broken, and people sin. Despite all of that, God is good.

But don't just take my word for it. Accept David's invitation and experience God's goodness for yourself:

> Taste and see that the LORD is good. Oh, the joys of those who take refuge in him! (Psalm 34:8)

The more you learn about God's character and grow in your relationship (by walking and talking with Him each day like you would your best friend), the more you will see and experience the goodness of God for yourself. Taste, and you will see!

<< ASK >>

When are you most tempted to doubt God's goodness?

List three good things about who God is and what He's done for you.

1.

2.

3.

<< PRAY >>

Father God, I praise You today for being my good and faithful God. Open my eyes so that I can see Your goodness all around me. Even when life is hard, remind me that You are good, and continue to grow in me a faith that relies wholeheartedly on You.

<< LIVE >>

We get good at the things we practice, so this week let's practice looking for the goodness of God all around us in two specific ways:

- Look for the good in people (even the ones who are generally difficult, unkind, or annoying). Every person is made in the image of God, so they have good inside them. We just have to be willing to search for the good.

- Look for the good in your circumstances (even the ones that are "hard" or "bad"). Tell God that no matter what, you want to trust Him, and ask Him to show you how He's working all things for good.

He is ...
IN CONTROL, ALL-POWERFUL, & GOOD.

Look back over Lessons 10–12. What stuck out to you? Did you learn something new? What is one truth you want to remember about God this week?

<< READ IT >>
- ☐ 1 Chronicles 29:10–13
- ☐ Psalm 107:1, 8–9
- ☐ James 1:17

<< WRITE IT >>

Look up Jeremiah 32:17. Write the verse in the space provided.

<< SHARE IT >>

Share with someone the one big truth you learned about God this week. Who are you going to tell? _____
(Now go do it!)

WEEK FIVE

GOD ALMIGHTY

#13 He is ...
ALL-SUFFICIENT

(God Almighty: El Shaddai)

When Abram was ninety-nine years old, the LORD appeared to him and said, "I am El-Shaddai — 'God Almighty.' Serve me faithfully and live a blameless life." (Genesis 17:1)

Let's start today with a question: Do you think it's possible for us to obey every command in the Bible? Or to put it another way: Do you think God requires impossible things from us?

Take our key verse, for example. When Abram (who was later renamed Abraham) was 99 years old, God commanded him to walk before Him faithfully and be blameless (NIV). Basically, God was telling Abram that He wanted him to live his life (or walk) continually in God's presence and be perfect (or blameless). Was God setting Abram up for failure with an impossible command? The answer is yes ... and no.

Yes, it's true. The Bible is filled with commands that we have no hope of fulfilling on our own. To be clear, there's not one command that you and I are able to perfectly follow on our own. Not even one. Therefore, in response to both His standard and our need, God chose to reveal Himself as God Almighty, the English translation for the Hebrew name *El Shaddai,* which means "All-Sufficient One, the One Who Satisfies."

Although the world tries to convince us that we are capable of anything and that in and of ourselves we are enough, the truth is we aren't. We all have limitations that leave us lacking. No one is without weakness and inadequacy. Apart from God, we can do nothing (John 15:5).

But notice in our key verse that God doesn't ask if Abram is able to do what is being asked. Instead, God begins by telling Abram who He is. He says (my paraphrase): "I'm God Almighty — the All-Sufficient One. I will be the answer to your every need. Now walk before Me and be blameless."

God doesn't disappear after calling us to walk before Him, crossing His fingers and hoping we can figure out how to live our lives on our own. His desire for us isn't greater independence — it's greater dependence. He wants us to learn to live completely dependent on Him for everything we do.

So, back to our question: Does God require impossible things from us? No, because He offers Himself as the answer to our every need. God Almighty will always and forever be enough for us.

<< ASK >>

The word *sufficient* means "enough, plenty, abundant." What do you think it means for God to call Himself the All-Sufficient One?

Why do you think God wants us to become more dependent on Him, not more independent?

<< PRAY >>

Heavenly Father, thank You for revealing Yourself today as God Almighty. Teach me how to live each day more dependent on You. I want to learn to trust that You are enough for me.

<< LIVE >>

Think through the many different areas of your life: family, friendships, dating relationships, school, work, church, sports, extracurricular activities. How can you depend on God more in every area of your life?

#14 He is ...
SATISFYING

(God Almighty: El Shaddai)

Let them praise the LORD for his great love and for the wonderful things he has done for them. For he satisfies the thirsty and fills the hungry with good things. (Psalm 107:8–9)

Every person in this world wants to find true happiness and contentment. It's built into how we were made. By design, God placed in each one of us the need to be satisfied — to be filled deep down inside. In church lingo, we use words like "hunger" and "thirst" to describe our need. But all that means is this: We all have a longing to be filled — to find that something or someone that will truly satisfy all the desires of our heart.

From an early age, we start looking for things that we think will fill us up. Usually that looking starts with thinking that *stuff* will make us happy. Can you remember when you thought your life would be made if you finally got that American Girl doll, a new bike, or the latest video game? Or maybe it was the latest and greatest new phone. We thought those things would satisfy us — and maybe they did for a little while — but eventually we wanted more. Now that you're older, you've probably moved on to looking for satisfaction in other ways, like getting good grades, becoming the star athlete, or finding the perfect significant other. But guess what? Those things will leave you wanting, too.

Here's the good news: When God introduced Himself as God Almighty, He was revealing Himself as the "All-Sufficient One" *and* the "One Who Satisfies." So, that deep hole inside you that needs to be filled, that God-given desire to be satisfied — it can only be met by God Himself. Only God can satisfy every desire of our heart. *Only* God.

Everywhere we turn, something or someone is promising to satisfy us — to fill us — but they all fall short. There will always be someone smarter and more talented than you. Even if you accomplish your greatest achievement or most challenging goal, there will always be another (higher) mountain to climb. And no relationship, no matter how great the love, will ever meet your every need. There is no job, no amount of money, no perfect family, and no perfect future that will fill you up. Only Jesus satisfies. Only God Almighty is enough. Everything else is a rotten substitute.

<< ASK >>

When you were little, what was that one thing you just had to have to be happy?

How would you describe to a friend what it means to spiritually hunger and thirst?

What are some of the things you hope will satisfy you in your life right now?

<< PRAY >>

Father God, thank You for revealing Yourself as God Almighty, the only One who satisfies. Make me aware throughout the day of all the other people, places, and things I run to for satisfaction apart from You. And anytime I feel that hunger rising, teach me how to turn my heart to You.

<< LIVE >>

Most of the time, we look to other people, places, and things to make us happy because we want instant gratification (or a quick fix). We assume that seeking God to meet all our needs will take too much time and/or be too much work, but it doesn't have to. Sometimes turning to Jesus can be as simple as our next breath.

Today, we're going to practice "breath prayers." A *breath prayer* is a simple, quick way to turn your heart and mind to the Lord throughout your day. This is how it works:

1. Choose a couple words or a short phrase that you can use to connect with God. I'll list a few examples, but you choose one that's right for you.

    I need You, God.
    Thank You, Jesus.
    I trust You, Lord.
    Not my will, but Yours be done.
    More of You, less of me.
    Help me, Father.
    Jesus, You are enough for me.
    Jesus, let me feel Your love.

2. Throughout the day, when you feel a need arise, take a deep breath, and as you exhale, breathe out your prayer to the Lord.

Making these little connections with God all day long will guide your heart and mind to Jesus, the only One who can truly satisfy.

#15 He is ...
ENOUGH

(God Almighty: El Shaddai)

Each time he said, "My grace is all you need. My power works best in weakness." So now I am glad to boast about my weaknesses, so that the power of Christ can work through me. (2 Corinthians 12:9)

Before we move on to another name, there's one more thing about God Almighty that you should know. While some names of God are only referenced once or twice in the Bible, *El Shaddai* (or God Almighty) is found 48 times, and 31 of those are in the Book of Job.

Job, the Book, tells the story of Job, the man, who depended on God when everything in his life went terribly wrong (and trust me, *everything* in his life went *terribly* wrong!). But it was in those hard places, when Job came to the end of himself and hit rock-bottom, that God chose to reveal Himself as God Almighty. He will do the same for us too, if we're willing to seek Him.

The key verse you read above was written by the apostle Paul. Three times he asked God to remove from him a specific struggle, but God offered Himself as the answer instead. Let's read our key verse again in a different translation, and this time including the verse that follows:

> But the Lord said, "My grace is all you need. Only when you are weak can everything be done completely by my power." So I will gladly boast about my weaknesses. Then Christ's power can stay in me. Yes, I am glad to have weaknesses if they are for Christ. I am glad to be insulted and have hard times. I am glad when I am persecuted and have problems, because it is when I am

weak that I am really strong. (2 Corinthians 12:9–10 ERV)

Paul learned that it was only when he felt weak and incapable that God's grace (the gift of His enough-ness) became real to him. Do you know what that means? It means that if we want to experience God's enough-ness like Paul did, you and I are going to have to come face-to-face with our faults, weaknesses, and hardships. And if we're being honest, that's not an easy thing to do.

When it comes to our weaknesses, most of us would rather put on our strong face or sweep them under a rug. However, if we want to experience God at work in our lives, then we can't brush past our weaknesses. We can't keep trying to cover them, bandage them up, or fix them on our own. Instead, we need to learn to seek God in our weakness. When we do, we will find that He is enough for us, for His power is made perfect in our weakness.

‹‹ ASK ››

What is your usual response when you run into something you can't do or something that's hard for you? (Check all that apply.)

☐ Pretend like nothing is wrong
☐ Feel embarrassed and ashamed
☐ Put on my tough face and deal with it
☐ Shut down
☐ Ignore it
☐ Other _____

When life gets hard and you are forced to face your weakness, whom or what do you usually turn to for answers or help?

<< PRAY >>

Heavenly Father, thank You for promising to be enough for me. Although it's scary to admit my failures and acknowledge my needs, help me to learn to turn to and trust in You. I choose to believe today that my weaknesses will become the very places where I experience Your enough-ness at work within me.

<< LIVE >>

Although it may seem backwards, in God's eyes your weaknesses are actually the places of your greatest strength because that's where you'll learn to depend on Him most. Are you feeling weak today? Are there any areas of your life where you're really struggling? If so, rest today in the fact that God's grace is (and always will be) enough for you.

He is ...
ALL-SUFFICIENT, SATISFYING, & ENOUGH.

Look back over Lessons 13–15. What stuck out to you? Did you learn something new? What is one truth you want to remember about God this week?

<< READ IT >>

☐ John 15:1–8
☐ 2 Corinthians 4:7–9

<< WRITE IT >>

Look up John 10:10. Write the verse in the space provided.

<< SHARE IT >>

Share with someone the one big truth you learned about God this week. Who are you going to tell? _____ (Now go do it!)

WEEK SIX

THE LORD MY SHEPHERD

#16 He is ...

OUR HELPER

(The LORD My Shepherd: Jehovah Raah)

The LORD is my shepherd; I have all that I need. (Psalm 23:1)

Throughout the Bible, we are often referred to as sheep — an analogy that until recently I never understood. Having spent very little time among those white, woolly creatures (okay, zero time), I have drastically misunderstood and therefore taken for granted the name *Jehovah Raah,* or The LORD My Shepherd.

After doing some research, I learned that to understand the importance and value of God as my Shepherd, I needed to learn a few things about sheep. So, welcome to *Sheep-ology 101.*

For starters, you need to know that sheep are famous for being the dumbest of animals. They are easily lost when they wander off (which happens regularly) and have a hard time finding home, even when home is within sight. Sheep don't learn from their mistakes, so they do the same stupid things over and over again.

Sheep are extremely vulnerable animals. They have no ability to take care of themselves and are in need of constant, meticulous care. They also have poor instincts and no ability to protect or defend themselves. If a sheep falls over on its back, there's a good chance it will panic and die. And if that's not bad enough, sheep have been known to eat themselves right off a cliff while grazing.

Are you getting the picture now? Sheep are painfully high-maintenance, but their "diva" nature is no fault of their own. They were created that way. Sheep were made to need the help of a shepherd, and the same is true for you and me. Like sheep, you and I were created to need the tender care of a Shepherd. And if we're being honest, we need His help every minute of every day. This isn't something to resist or be ashamed of — it's how we were created. God, in His infinite wisdom and profound goodness, hardwired us to need His help, then He reaches out His hand and provides for us all the help we need.

What do you need help with today? Look no further than the helping hand of your Good Shepherd. He will be everything you need.

<< ASK >>

Go back and reread the description of sheep. Write down three ways you are like a sheep.

1.

2.

3.

Do you ever feel bad (or guilty) for asking God for help? If we were really created to need help, why do you think we so often feel bad asking?

<< PRAY >>

Father God, thank You for being my Good Shepherd. Teach me how to depend on You as my helper just like a sheep depends on its shepherd. Whether my need is big or small, I want to learn to turn to and trust in You.

<< LIVE >>

God wants to be involved in every part of our lives, both big and small. This week, let God participate (and help you) with *all the things,* and remember — He created you to need His help, so let Him, okay?!?

#17 He is ...
OUR GUIDE

(The LORD My Shepherd: Jehovah Raah)

He guides me along right paths, bringing honor to his name.
(Psalm 23:3b)

Who do you usually turn to when you don't know what to do? Have you ever wished that God would write in the sky the answer to a decision you're facing? Or maybe He could shape the clouds into arrows to show you which way to go? With so many of life's big decisions ahead of you, it's important to know that you can trust *Jehovah Raah,* The LORD My Shepherd, to guide you.

After all, knowing how to guide sheep comes with the role of a shepherd. A good shepherd has to know how to guide his flock. Because his sheep depend on him, the shepherd would never simply bark orders to his sheep, send them off, and wish them well. Instead, he always walks with his sheep to show them the way to go. This is one of my favorite things about our Good Shepherd — He promises to go with us. You and I don't have to be stressed or worried about what path to take in life. We just need to learn to listen for our Shepherd's voice and follow Him.

So, how do we do that? How do we know that we are following our Good Shepherd and not some other voice? Jesus explains it this way in the Gospel of John:

> The gatekeeper opens the gate for [the shepherd], and the sheep recognize his voice and come to him. He calls his own sheep by name and leads them out. After he has gathered his own flock, he walks ahead of them, and they follow him because they know his voice. (John 10:3–4)

At night, sheep were often gathered into a sheep pen with other flocks to protect them from thieves, weather, and wild animals. When it came time to leave the pen, each shepherd would call for his own flock, and his sheep would follow. As dumb as they were, sheep could always recognize, know, and follow the voice of their shepherd.

Do you know what this means? It means Jesus has a voice that you and I can know personally. Just like we can recognize the voice of those closest to us without seeing them, God's voice is one we can learn to recognize (and follow), too.

The more time you spend with God by reading the Bible and talking to Him, the more you will learn to distinguish and follow the voice of your Good Shepherd. You will find no better guide than Him. God's Word guaranteed!

> The LORD says, "I will guide you along the best pathway for your life. I will advise you and watch over you." (Psalm 32:8)

<< ASK >>

What's the one thing you want God's guidance for in your life right now?

Does knowing that you can know God's voice by reading His Word give you a desire to read it more? (Circle one) Yes or No

If your honest answer is "No," then a good place for you to start may be to begin asking God for the desire to know Him more through His Word. God delights in answering that kind of prayer!

<< PRAY >>

Father God, thank You for the ever-present, guiding hand of The LORD My Shepherd. Please give me the desire to read the Bible so I can learn to recognize Your voice. I want to learn to trust and follow You.

<< LIVE >>

Although this may sound old school, I encourage you to start reading from a real (paper) Bible instead of a little, glowing screen (such as a phone, computer, or iPad). I believe there's something powerful about opening the Bible to read God's Word from actual paper pages. Plus, we may become more interested in reading the verses surrounding the ones we initially started with when we're reading from an open book instead of a digital copy.

If you don't have a Bible, go get one this week! There are many different Bible translations to choose from. In this book, we've referenced the NLT (New Living Translation), NIV (New International Version), and ERV (Easy-to-Read Version). Any of those would be a good option for you.

And remember, learning to hear God's voice takes time. Just like all relationships, you won't acquire an ear for His voice overnight, and it won't happen by accident. However, over time, God will reveal Himself to you. You can trust that time spent in your Bible will never be wasted.

#18 He is ...
OUR PROTECTOR

(The LORD My Shepherd: Jehovah Raah)

Even when I walk through the darkest valley, I will not be afraid, for you are close beside me. Your rod and your staff protect and comfort me. (Psalm 23:4)

The last characteristic of The LORD My Shepherd we're going to focus on this week is God's role as our protector. Again, like we talked about in the last lesson, just as guiding is part of a shepherd's job description, so is protecting. A shepherd is expected to protect his sheep.

Let's look at two specific ways a shepherd protects his sheep based on our key verse from Psalm 23.

1. A good shepherd stays close to his sheep. The importance and value of the shepherd's constant presence cannot be stressed enough. Sheep are stressed, helpless, and lost without a shepherd. But under the protective care of their shepherd, a sheep can live without fear.

2. A good shepherd uses a rod and staff to protect his sheep. A rod is a thick stick with a club at the end. A shepherd uses the rod to nudge and redirect sheep back on path, to steer them away from danger, and to protect them from animal attacks. A staff is a long, skinny pole with a crook at the end (that happens to fit perfectly around a sheep's neck). The staff is used to lift the sheep out of harm's way. If a sheep is caught in thick brush or falls into a hole or deep water, a shepherd can reach down and scoop the sheep safely out of danger. Both tools are invaluable in the care and protection of the sheep.

Now let's talk about us. How does God protect us like a shepherd? First, God promises to always be with us. It's not only what He does, but who He is, remember? God will never leave your side — He will never abandon you. Not even death can separate us from the God who loves us more than we can imagine.

> Yes, I am sure that nothing can separate us from God's love — not death, life, angels, or ruling spirits. I am sure that nothing now, nothing in the future, no powers, nothing above us or nothing below us — nothing in the whole created world — will ever be able to separate us from the love God has shown us in Christ Jesus our Lord. (Romans 8:38–39 ERV)

God's presence changes everything! You and I can rest today knowing that with the God of the universe by our side, we have nothing to fear.

Second, although God doesn't literally carry around a rod and a staff, we can be sure that the Lord is continually nudging, redirecting, and steering our hearts and minds away from danger. He fights off outside attacks we never see coming and is careful to reach down and scoop us up when we fall into trouble.

Because of His never-ending love for you, you can trust that God will always be beside you to help, guide, and protect you. It's the way of the Good Shepherd.

<< ASK >>

Everyone struggles with fear. What are some of the biggest things that you fear?

How do you think trusting in God as the Good Shepherd can help you conquer your fears?

Can you think of a time when God nudged, redirected, or steered your heart and/or mind away from danger? Did the nudging come from inside you (by the Holy Spirit), or did He use someone else to nudge you? Share about it here.

<< PRAY >>

Father God, I praise You today for being my Good Shepherd. Thank You for promising to always be by my side to protect and comfort me. Teach me every day how to overcome my fears by trusting in You, The LORD My Shepherd.

<< LIVE >>

Have you ever noticed how big and bossy your fears can be? This week, practice telling your fears how big your God is! It's time to put our fears in their proper place.

He is ...
OUR HELPER, GUIDE, & PROTECTOR.

Look back over Lessons 16–18. What stuck out to you? Did you learn something new? What is one truth you want to remember about God this week?

<< READ IT >>
- ☐ Psalm 23
- ☐ Psalm 121
- ☐ John 10:1–15

<< WRITE IT >>

Look up John 10:14–15. Write the verse in the space provided.

<< SHARE IT >>

Share with someone the one big truth you learned about God this week. Who are you going to tell? _____
(Now go do it!)

WEEK SEVEN

THE LORD PROVIDES

#19 He is ...

PROVIDER

(The LORD Provides: Jehovah Jireh)

... for your Father knows exactly what you need even before you ask him! (Matthew 6:8b)

Do you know anyone who is a constant worrier? Maybe it's your mom, your grandma, a teacher, or a close friend. Or maybe the biggest worrier is you! Although some think worrying is just for adults, I'm pretty sure you can give me a long list of worries, too. Do you ever worry about your grades, family stress, what people think of you, how to cover that big zit on your forehead, a lack of time to get everything done, your body image, your future, or if you'll ever get a date?

While these might be normal things to worry about, it's important to understand that God never intended us to live in worry (or fear). That's why, in the Book of Genesis, He is introduced by another very important name, *Jehovah Jireh*. As we've already learned, the name *Jehovah,* or *Yahweh,* is the Hebrew word for LORD. *Jireh* means "to see, to see beforehand." (It's where we get our word "provision.") Put together, the compound name *Jehovah Jireh* is translated as "The LORD Provides."

Are you wondering how this name relates to worrying? When God revealed Himself as the Provider, He wanted us to know we don't have to worry anymore because we have a God who knows our needs better than we know them ourselves. He sees our needs before we even realize we have a need and promises to provide for us. Amazing, right?

In Matthew's Gospel, Jesus says: "I tell you not to worry" (Matthew 6:25). Then He points us to the birds of the air and the lilies of the field, who are perfectly provided for by the Lord, as proof that God is a trustworthy and abundant Provider. If God provides for them, how much more will He provide for you and me? And then, He says ...

> "So don't worry about these things, saying, 'What will we eat? What will we drink? What will we wear?' These things dominate the thoughts of unbelievers, but your heavenly Father already knows all your needs. (Matthew 6:31–32)

Have your thoughts ever been dominated by worry? Mine have! Here's how I'd paraphrase the verse above: "Worry? That's what the godless do! That's what those *without* a God do. But you ... child, you have a God in heaven who loves you — who knows what you need before you ask — who sees your need before it even arises and makes provision for it. His name is The LORD Provides, so do not worry."

Although worry has become a normal part of living, it doesn't change the fact that worry is a sin. It's a sign of misplaced trust. When we worry, we take God out of the picture — we imagine our problems, our situation, or our life without God. But that's not our reality, nor will it ever be! So, let's decide today to take God at His Word and trust Him as our Provider. And let's decide to be done with worry for good!

<< ASK >>

What are some of the things you worry about on a regular basis?

When we worry, we're telling God that He's not big enough, strong enough, or capable enough to take care of us. How does this perspective-change affect the way you view worry?

<< PRAY >>

Heavenly Father, thank You for revealing Yourself as my Provider. Forgive me for all the times I worry and stress instead of trusting in You to provide for me. I don't want to worry anymore, Lord. Teach me how to turn all my worries and fears over to You.

<< LIVE >>

Here's the problem for most of us: We've made a habit of worry. It's our natural reflex to life's trouble and stress. To get rid of this habit, we need to replace worrying with something new. So, next time worry pops into your head, retrain your mind to think about God. Ask yourself: Where is God in this concerning situation? Invite Him back into the picture in your mind. And remember, you are never without our good and faithful God. The more you allow God to re-enter the scene, the more your worries and fears will begin to disappear. Try it this week!

#20 He is …

NEVER LATE

(The LORD Provides: Jehovah Jireh)

We wait in hope for the LORD; he is our help and our shield. In him our hearts rejoice, for we trust in his holy name.
(Psalm 33:20–21 NIV)

Do you want to know one of my least favorite four-letter words? It's WAIT. Anyone else? Waiting is hard! I don't like waiting in lines, waiting on my people, or waiting for my turn. And let's face it — waiting on God is hard, too.

What do we do when we go to God with our requests, trusting Him alone for provision, but His answer comes like a blinking neon sign that reads, "Wait!"? Sometimes God seems downright slow — slow to hear, slow to answer, and slow to deliver. As much as we want to trust God as our Provider, waiting on Him isn't easy.

The struggle is real, but it isn't new. The Bible is filled with stories of people who had a hard time waiting on God. Like us, they had to learn that trusting in God as Provider means learning to trust in His timing, too. So, how do we learn to wait well?

The word *wait* means "to hope for, look for, expect, have full confidence in." Is this how we usually wait on the Lord, in confident expectation that our provision is coming?

Imagine that your family finally booked that dream vacation you've been talking about for years. You think, "It's finally going to happen!" as you pull out your calendar and circle the date in red. As days and months fly by, you cross off squares on your calendar. (Wait, does anyone use a paper calendar anymore?) Anticipation grows. Every day that passes is one less day to wait. When the day finally arrives, you're so excited. You never doubted for a second that the vacation wouldn't happen. The trip will be well worth the wait!

Now insert those things that you've been waiting on God for. Do we wait on God like that? With anticipation growing and excitement building? Like each day that passes is one less day to wait? Although we can't circle a date on a calendar or count down the days, we have a God in heaven who is faithful. His calendar is marked, and His plans cannot be spoiled.

God's delay in provision is not His denial. He hasn't forgotten about you, and He's not running late. He's actively aware of every detail of your need, and He's working, in His time and according to His good and perfect plan. Although we don't always understand it, we can rest in knowing that God's timing will (somehow) be perfect. He is never, ever late.

> Yet I am confident I will see the LORD's goodness while I am here in the land of the living. Wait patiently for the LORD. Be brave and courageous. Yes, wait patiently for the LORD. (Psalm 27:13–14)

<< ASK >>

Think of a time you had to wait for something you really wanted. How did you feel as you waited?

Is there something you've asked God for and you're still waiting for His answer? What is it?

<< PRAY >>

Father God, I'll be the first to admit that waiting is hard. Most of the time I want what I want when I want it. But, Lord, as I begin to trust in You more as my Provider, I pray that You'd give me a faith that not only trusts in Your provision but also trusts in Your timing. I believe today that You're always working on my behalf, and You're never late.

<< LIVE >>

Think about what you look like when you're waiting. What's your body posture? What's your attitude?

Many times, I admit, my waiting looks like me sitting on the ground right where I am, arms crossed, and finger tapping, "Come on, God. I'm waiting."

But that's not the picture the Scripture paints of waiting. The root word for *wait* in the Bible gives a picture of tying a knot or binding together, usually by twisting. Maybe this picture means that God's intention for us during times of waiting is for us to learn how to live so dependently on Him that we are bound together, twisted in an inseparable knot.

Next time you're waiting for something, instead of crossing your arms (because waiting is hard and inconvenient), think about twisting up with God because you trust Him as your good and faithful Provider.

#21 He is …

THE ANSWER

(The LORD Provides: Jehovah Jireh)

And this same God who takes care of me will supply all your needs from his glorious riches, which have been given to us in Christ Jesus. (Philippians 4:19)

Did you know that every single person who has ever walked the face of this earth has the same primary need? Although it may not be something we think about regularly, this need relates to a universal problem we all experience every day — the problem of sin.

> For everyone has sinned; we all fall short of God's glorious standard. (Romans 3:23)

In his letter to the Romans, the apostle Paul points out that every one of us has sinned — we all fall short of the perfect and holy standard of God. Because of our sin, we've all been separated from God and sentenced to death (Romans 6:23). I know it sounds harsh, but don't worry — there's good news.

Because of His great love for us, while we were still sinners, our Provider sent His Son, Jesus, to die for us (Romans 5:8). God doesn't wait for us to be good enough to earn His forgiveness, and He doesn't expect us to clean up our act or start following a bunch of rules before He'll save us. Instead, He meets us where we are, sees the mess that we're in (sees our need), and sends Jesus to provide for us.

When Jesus died on the cross all those years ago, He died for all the sins of all the people for all time (and included in that "all" are you and me). Jesus is God's greatest provision for us. He is both the Provider and the provision. He is the answer to our biggest need.

I want you to read our key verse for today again, but this time in a different translation.

> My God will use his glorious riches to give you everything you need. He will do this through Christ Jesus. (Philippians 4:19 ERV)

If God, through Jesus, can provide for your biggest need (by defeating sin and death), what need is too big for Him? What problem is too great? My friends, Jesus is the answer to everything you need, today, tomorrow, and always. Will you trust Him today?

<< ASK >>

How do you define sin?

How often do you think about your sin?

Describe in your own words how God made provision for our biggest need.

<< PRAY >>

Heavenly Father, thank You not only for being my Provider but also for offering Yourself as the provision (the answer) to my greatest need. It's hard for me to understand all the ways You love me and the amazing sacrifice You made for me personally. Thank You for being the answer to my every need, and thank You for helping me to trust You.

<< LIVE >>

There's a big difference between believing in Jesus and His life-saving gift and receiving it personally. If you have yet to receive this gift of life through a personal relationship with Jesus, don't wait another day. God has made provision for you.

Pray with me.

> God, thank You for loving me and sending Jesus to die on the cross for my sins. Today I choose to receive the gift of Your forgiveness by placing my faith in You. Teach me how to trust You for everything I need as I begin my relationship with You.

If you prayed this prayer for the first time today, tell a trusted friend or mentor, and let him or her celebrate with you. We should never walk the life of faith alone.

He is ...
PROVIDER,
NEVER LATE,
& THE ANSWER.

Look back over Lessons 19–21. What stuck out to you? Did you learn something new? What is one truth you want to remember about God this week?

<< READ IT >>
- ☐ Matthew 6:25–34
- ☐ Mark 6:30–44
- ☐ Romans 5:6–8

<< WRITE IT >>

Look up 2 Peter 1:3. Write the verse in the space provided.

<< SHARE IT >>

Share with someone the one big truth you learned about God this week. Who are you going to tell? _____
(Now go do it!)

WEEK EIGHT

THE LORD HEALS

#22 He is ...

OUR HEALER

(The LORD Heals: Jehovah Rapha)

"LORD, help!" they cried in their trouble, and he saved them from their distress. He sent out his word and healed them, snatching them from the door of death. (Psalm 107:19–20)

Raise your hand if you've ever been stuck in bed sick or had to sit on the sidelines of a game because of an injury? We don't have to look far to see our need for healing. Just take a quick drive around town and you'll see either a doctor's office, pharmacy, or emergency care facility on almost every street corner. In a world that's filled with illness, disease, and pain, we need to know we have somewhere or someone to turn to for healing.

Throughout the pages of the New Testament, we read countless stories of how Jesus gave sight to the blind, made the lame to walk, healed disease, and even raised the dead. But what about now? Does God still heal today?

Our answer lies in another one of God's names, *Jehovah Rapha,* The LORD Heals. One of the first things we learned about the Lord is that He is constant, unchanging. So that means the same God we read about in the pages of our Bible is still healing today.

Like most Hebrew words, the word *rapha* means much more than "to heal." Listen to the full definition: "to heal, repair, purify, restore, recover, refresh, relieve, cure, make whole." You and I don't have to be physically sick to be in need of a healer. Do you have any relationships that are in need of *repair?* Do you have any thoughts or motives that need *purifying?* Would you like the Lord to *refresh* any crushed hopes or dreams? Are you looking for some *relief* from your worries or stress? Would you like to be *made whole?* All of these are included in the work of our Healer.

And there's one more thing. The word picture for the Hebrew word *rapha* is one of something (or someone) being sewn back together. Think about what an up-close-and-personal thing this is — to be held in the Father's hand while you are being mended back together.

Next time you or a loved one is in need of healing (whether it's physical, emotional, spiritual, mental, or moral healing), turn to the Lord, cry out for His help, and rest in His hand. He is your Healer.

<< A∫K >>

Instead of asking you questions today, I'm going to answer some questions that may have surfaced as you read. What about when healing doesn't come? What about those times when we ask God to heal someone and they still pass away? Where is our Healer then?

My answer: He was there, listening to every word you prayed and catching every tear. God didn't turn His back on you *or* your loved one. For believers, healing came for them, perfectly and completely, in heaven.

Revelation 21:4 says this about heaven: "He [Jesus] will wipe every tear from their eyes, and there will be no more death or sorrow or crying or pain. All these things are gone forever."

I don't know why we don't receive all of our healing on this side of eternity, but I do know our God is only and always good. Life and death are in His hands, and He can be trusted, even when we don't understand. His ways are higher than ours, and they are always right and just. You and I live in a fallen and broken land, ravaged by sin, sickness, and pain, but we are not left on our own.

Our Healer walks with us. He is always present and always healing. Will you lean in and believe?

<< PRAY >>

Father God, help us to learn to turn to You as our Healer. Even when we don't understand your ways, remind us that we can trust You, for You alone are faithful, just, right, and good. We praise You today for all the ways You've already healed us and for all the healing You have yet to do.

<< LIVE >>

Read Psalm 103:1–5. We often forget to thank God for all the things He does for us. Like David in this psalm, spend a few minutes listing (and praising) God for His many benefits, including some of the ways that He's already healed you.

#23 He is …

OUR COMFORTER

(The LORD Heals: Jehovah Rapha)

All praise to God, the Father of our Lord Jesus Christ. God is our merciful Father and the source of all comfort. (2 Corinthians 1:3)

Some days life just feels hard, doesn't it? No one travels through life without feeling heartache, sorrow, and grief. We all go through difficult times and experience different kinds of suffering. So today, as we continue to look to God as The LORD Heals, we're going to focus on how sometimes God's healing comes to us through His comfort.

In our key verse, the apostle Paul names God as our merciful Father and the source of all comfort. Paul, an apostle who went through far more than his fair share of trials and suffering, points to God alone as his source of comfort. (Remember talking about God as our Source in Lesson #1?) Is this how you view God, too — as the source of all your comfort?

If I'm being honest, God isn't always the first one who comes to mind when I'm feeling sad or heartbroken. I usually want someone close to me (someone with skin on) to sit by my side and say all the right words to make me feel better (and they get bonus points if they come with candy or a large bowl of ice cream). But the truth is that no one can truly heal our heartaches, except God.

> He heals the brokenhearted and bandages their wounds. (Psalm 147:3)

Here's another truth you can depend on: Anytime you are brokenhearted, hurt, or suffering, God is already with you, ready and able to supply all the comfort you will ever need. He doesn't just give you *a little bit* of comfort so that you'll feel *a little better* for *a little while*. No — He gives you *all* the comfort you need *every* time you need it. All we have to do is cry out to Him — He is the source of all comfort.

> O my people, trust in him at all times. Pour out your heart to him, for God is our refuge. (Psalm 62:8)

Picture God standing by your side with His ever-present arm protectively wrapped around your shoulder. This God of ours is both tender and strong. As you learn to lean on Him, He will comfort you, take your sorrow, and heal your wounds as He encourages and strengthens you.

<< ASK >>

When you are sad or brokenhearted, what is most comforting to you?

- ☐ When someone listens and talks to you about your pain
- ☐ When someone sits quietly with you
- ☐ A large bowl of ice cream
- ☐ Other _____

God comforts us in many different ways. How have you experienced the comfort of God? (For example, through prayer, by listening to music, through other people, through reading the Bible)

<< PRAY >>

Father God, thank You for promising to always be by my side to comfort and heal me. Remind me when I'm feeling low to turn my heart to You as my comforter. I want to learn to depend on You for everything I need.

<< LIVE >>

With God, no pain is ever wasted. Read 2 Corinthians 1:3–4. After God has comforted us, what does He want us to do?

Has God ever used you to comfort someone else in the same way He has comforted you? Write about it here.

All we have to do is pay attention and be available. God can and will use you to comfort those around you in the same personal way He has comforted you.

#24 He is ...

OUR REDEEMER

(The LORD Heals: Jehovah Rapha)

But he was pierced for our rebellion, crushed for our sins. He was beaten so we could be whole. He was whipped so we could be healed. (Isaiah 53:5)

We're going to end this week with one more important truth about our God: He is our Redeemer. *Redeem* isn't a word most of us use in our daily life, so let me define it for us. To redeem means "to buy or pay off; clear by payment, to buy back, to recover."

Remember in Lesson #21 when we talked about how God provided for our greatest need by sending Jesus to the cross to die for our sins? When Jesus was crucified, died, and was buried, He *redeemed* us from sin and the death penalty that came with it. As our key verse says, Jesus was punished for what *we* did. He was crushed because of *our* guilt. He took the punishment *we* deserved, and we were healed because of *his* pain. That's redemption!

But that's not the end of our redemption story, as incredible as it is. Let me explain by telling you the story about a man in the Bible named Joseph. Joseph was one of the 12 sons of Jacob. Actually, he was the favorite son of Jacob, and everybody knew it. Because of their jealousy, Joseph's brothers hated him and made plans to kill him. (Nice family, weren't they?) Thankfully, one of his brothers talked the other 10 out of murder, so the brothers beat Joseph, threw him in a pit, then sold him as a slave instead.

But that's not the end of Joseph's crazy story. Without going into all the details, Joseph was sold again, accused of something he didn't do, punished for doing what was right, put in jail, and forgotten by those he had helped. But through it all, God's invisible hand was at work. It was through this series of trials and misfortunes that Joseph found himself in the position to be elevated to second in command over all of Egypt.

God redeemed Joseph's life. Listen to how Joseph described his redemption:

> You intended to harm me, but God intended it all for good. He brought me to this position so I could save the lives of many people. (Genesis 50:20)

Joseph understood that God was able to redeem anything and everything in his life. He took what was meant for harm (or evil) and designed it for good. And He can do the same thing for me and you, too.

There is nothing in your life — no hardship, no trial, no struggle, no suffering, no sin, no tragedy, no relationship, no secret, no accusation, no reputation, no past — that God cannot redeem.

> And we know that God causes everything to work together for the good of those who love God and are called according to his purpose for them. (Romans 8:28)

Our God is a redeeming God. He takes our messes, our broken pieces, and our suffering and works all things together for our good. Will you trust Him today?

<< ASK >>

Define *redeem* in your own words.

Is there anything in your life right now that feels too broken, too ugly, or too painful to be redeemed? If so, what is it?

<< PRAY >>

Heavenly Father, I praise You today for being my Redeemer. Not only have You redeemed my life from sin, but You also promise to work all things in my life (even my mistakes, my past, my suffering, and my heartache) for good. Thank You for loving me, healing me, and redeeming me, today and always!

<< LIVE >>

God's redeeming work is often easier to recognize in hindsight. Take some time to think back on past mistakes, heartache, struggles, broken relationships, or suffering you've endured. List them here.

Can you see how God has been working to redeem (to recover or bring about good) those things from your past? If so, how? If not, ask Him to show you how He is working all things (including those things you listed) for your good.

He is ...
OUR HEALER,
COMFORTER,
& REDEEMER.

Look back over Lessons 22–24. What stuck out to you? Did you learn something new? What is one truth you want to remember about God this week?

<< READ IT >>
☐ Luke 4:16–21
☐ Luke 5:17–26

<< WRITE IT >>

Look up Isaiah 43:18–19. Write the verse in the space provided.

<< SHARE IT >>

Share with someone the one big truth you learned about God this week. Who are you going to tell? _____
(Now go do it!)

WEEK NINE

THE LORD MY BANNER

#25 He is …

OUR DEFENDER

(The LORD My Banner: Jehovah Nissi)

The LORD himself will fight for you. Just stay calm.
(Exodus 14:14)

Today I'm going to introduce you to another name of God, but this one requires a little more explaining for us to understand and apply. In ancient times, a banner (which is like our modern-day flag) was held at the army's front lines during times of battle. The banner was used to bring together and rally the troops before and during battle, reminding them whose side they were on and what they were fighting for. These banners were symbols of unity, strength, and protection.

God first revealed Himself as *Jehovah Nissi,* The LORD Is My Banner, in Exodus 17 when He gave the Israelite army victory over their enemy in the most unusual way. Here was their battle plan: Moses would send Joshua out to lead the army in battle while he stood on top of the hill with the staff of God (which was a symbol of God's presence and protection) in his hands. As long as Moses kept his hands up, the Israelites were winning. But when he lowered his hands, the enemy would take over. When Moses became too tired to stand, he sat on a rock while two of his men, Aaron and Hur, held up his hands, ensuring Israel's final victory.

Without question, everyone in that fight knew that their victory was because of God and God alone. It was His power, presence, and protection that went before them. He was their banner — their defender — the One who fought their battle for them.

So, my question for you today is this: What battles are you fighting right now? Do you have a friend at school who's talking behind your back or starting rumors about you? Are you struggling with a particular temptation that feels too overwhelming to resist? Do you constantly fight negative voices in your head? Are you beat down by what feels like constant rejection from someone who is important to you?

These are the battles that our Defender wants to fight for us. All God asks is that we look up to our Banner and trust Him.

> This is my command — be strong and courageous! Do not be afraid or discouraged. For the LORD your God is with you wherever you go. (Joshua 1:9)

When we stand under the banner of God, by staying under His love, truth, guidance, and protection, we can trust that He will fight for us. Take a deep breath, friend. This isn't your fight — the battle is the Lord's.

<< ASK >>

Have you ever thought about God wanting to fight your battles for you? (Circle one) Yes or No

What battle(s) would you like the Lord to fight for you right now?

We do not have to fight our battles alone. When Moses grew tired and couldn't hold his hands up any longer, he had friends there to step in and help him. Who is someone you can turn to for support when you're fighting your battles?

<< PRAY >>

Heavenly Father, thank You for revealing Yourself to me as my Banner. Remind me when I'm facing attacks or battles in my life that I don't face them alone. I want to learn to trust You as my Defender, Lord. Please fight my battles for me, I pray.

<< LIVE >>

God is always fighting our battles for us (whether we realize it or not), but we can learn to depend on Him more by talking to Him about our struggles and trusting Him to protect and defend us. Talk to God today about the battles you're facing, big or small. Thank Him for promising to go before you to fight for you, and trust Him to see you through. Our God is able!

#26 He is ...
OUR STRENGTH

(The LORD My Banner: Jehovah Nissi)

A final word: Be strong in the Lord and in his mighty power.
(Ephesians 6:10)

Who is the strongest person you know? Is the first person that comes to mind someone who is strong physically (like they can bench-press a ridiculous amount of weight or flex the biggest muscle)? Or are they strong emotionally (because they've walked through some really hard trials and come out better for it)?

There are many different kinds of strength needed to navigate this life well. And as our Banner, God promises that He will both *make us* strong and *be* our strength. What does that mean? How do we access and utilize God's supernatural power at work in our lives?

Our key verse for today tells us to be strong *in the Lord* and *in his power*. Strength from the Lord comes when we learn to turn to Him every time we have a need. When we call upon Him, He will supply (and be) all the strength we need.

> Search for the LORD and for his strength; continually seek him. (Psalm 105:4)

Have you ever wished you had more strength to face your daily struggles? Have you ever needed more strength to resist an overwhelming temptation, strength to stay awake and focus for that big test, strength to do the right thing, even when it's not the popular choice, strength to keep going when you want to give up, strength to experience joy when you're having a bad day, strength to have that hard conversation that you've been putting off, strength to trust God in what feels like an impossible situation, strength to ask for help when you're struggling, strength to be yourself instead of trying to fit in, or strength to wake up and face another day?

If you've ever felt like you had to be the strong one, you can rest easy today. God wants to be your strength. He wants you to learn to rely on Him so that He can work His power in and through you. Will you lean in and believe?

<< ASK >>

Who is the strongest person you know? Why?

What do you need God's strength for right now? (Feel free to borrow from the list in today's lesson if any of those relate to you.)

<< PRAY >>

Heavenly Father, I praise You today for being my strength. Remind me all throughout the day to turn my heart and mind to You for strength when I need it, and teach me how to be strong in Your mighty power, I pray.

<< LIVE >>

There is no one stronger than our God. Let Him be your strength for every need, big or small. Talk to God today about the needs you listed above and trust that He will give you all the strength you need.

#27 He is ...

OUR VICTORY

(The LORD My Banner: Jehovah Nissi)

For the LORD your God is going with you! He will fight for you against your enemies, and he will give you victory! (Deuteronomy 20:4)

The Old Testament is filled with stories of God's chosen people, the Israelites, and their many conquests and battles. And while we like to highlight the stories of their miraculous victories (like David taking down the giant, Goliath), it's important to know that the people of God didn't always win. There were times when they chose to disobey God and go their own way. During their times of rebellion, God's protective covering was removed and the nation not only suffered a loss, but also was forced to face the consequences of their disobedience.

As *Jehovah Nissi*, The LORD My Banner, God wasn't obligated to promote and/or bless the Israelite's selfish plans and purposes, but when they aligned themselves with His (God's plans and purposes), their victory was assured. One way or another, the Israelites learned their lesson: When you team up with God, you get the win.

So, what about us now? How is knowing God as The LORD My Banner relevant to us today? As followers of God in the 21st century, you and I stand under the banner of Jesus.

> But thank God! He gives us victory over sin and death through our Lord Jesus Christ. (1 Corinthians 15:57)

When Jesus was raised up on the cross, He defeated sin and death and, in doing so, secured our victory. So, like the Israelites all those years ago, when we team up with Jesus, we too will get the win. Similarly, when we step out from under the banner of Jesus, we're choosing to fight our battles on our own, too.

Try picturing God's banner like an umbrella. When you and I participate in our relationship with Jesus and make choices that reflect and honor Him, we're choosing to stay under the protection, provision, and victory of the Lord. But when we choose to go our own way or make choices that displease God (when we sin), we're choosing to step out from under His umbrella. This doesn't mean we're no longer saved (once saved, always saved), but we remove ourselves from His protective covering and His guaranteed victory.

The choice is ours. Whose banner will you stand under today?

<< ASK >>

What does it mean to you personally that we have victory over sin and death because of Jesus?

If God's banner is like an umbrella, where do you see yourself standing? (Are you safely under His covering, half in/half out and getting a little wet, or standing in the rain?)

If you picture yourself outside of the covering of His umbrella, what would it take for you to get back under the Banner of God?

<< PRAY >>

Father God, I praise You today for the victory You have given me in Jesus. I understand that when I choose to team up with You by aligning my heart and life to Your plans and purposes, You will give me victory. Please give me the courage and strength to choose well so that I stay under Your protective covering for all my days.

<< LIVE >>

God wants to give you victory in every area of your life, but He can't do that when you choose to live apart from Him. Think through the many aspects of your life. In what areas do you feel like you're aligned with God?

Are there any areas of life that you know you're choosing to go your own way? If so, what are they?

Are you willing to confess your selfish, independent ways and step back under the Banner of the Lord? If so, tell God today, and trust that He will receive you with open arms.

> But if we confess our sins, God will forgive us. We can trust God to do this. He always does what is right. He will make us clean from all the wrong things we have done. (1 John 1:9 ERV)

He is ...

OUR DEFENDER, STRENGTH, & VICTORY.

Look back over Lessons 25–27. What stuck out to you? Did you learn something new? What is one truth you want to remember about God this week?

<< READ IT >>

- ☐ Exodus 17:8–16
- ☐ Ephesians 6:10–18
- ☐ Romans 8:31–39

<< WRITE IT >>

Look up Romans 8:31. Write the verse in the space provided.

<< SHARE IT >>

Share with someone the one big truth you learned about God this week. Who are you going to tell? _____
(Now go do it!)

THE LORD WHO SANCTIFIES

#28 He is ...

HOLY

(The LORD Who Sanctifies: Jehovah Mekadesh)

No one is holy like the LORD! There is no one besides you; there is no Rock like our God. (1 Samuel 2:2)

We're ending our last week together with the single most important characteristic of God: He is holy. God's holiness both defines and encompasses all of His other character traits.

Holiness is defined as "morally perfect, pure, and set apart from sin." The holiness of God is what sets Him apart from (and above) everything and everyone else. In the Old Testament, when men encountered the holiness of God, they ended up on their knees with their faces flat on the floor. The Lord's greatness, mystery, and power are more than we can handle or endure.

It's in the understanding of His holiness, however, that God revealed yet another one of His many names, *Jehovah Mekadesh,* The LORD Who Sanctifies. In the Book of Leviticus, God issued this command to the nation of Israel:

> So set yourselves apart to be holy, for I am the LORD your God. Keep all my decrees by putting them into practice, for I am the LORD who makes you holy. (Leviticus 20:7–8)

There are two important truths we need to understand from these verses.

1. God commands His chosen people to be holy. When God called the Israelites to be His chosen nation, He was calling them to a new way of living. He was setting them apart from the ways of the world for His special plans

and purposes. God wants His people to look like Him — He was calling them to reflect the God they served. God is holy, so His people should be holy, too.

2. God then tells them that He will sanctify them — He will make them holy. Remember in Lesson #13 when we talked about how God is all-sufficient? We learned that God often expects the impossible from us, then offers Himself as the answer and means for the impossible. That's what He's doing here. God commands His people to be holy (hello — impossible!!), then tells them that He will sanctify them (or make them holy).

So, again, how does this Old Testament command relate to us? Because God is the same yesterday, today, and forever, His command to us today is no different from His command to the people of Israel. The apostle Peter reminds us:

> But now you must be holy in everything you do, just as God who chose you is holy. For the Scriptures say, "You must be holy because I am holy." (1 Peter 1:15–16)

God's command to His chosen ones (which includes you and me) hasn't changed after all these years: Be holy because I am holy. God wants His followers to look like Him (He wants us to reflect the God we serve) so that He can use us to accomplish His holy plans and purposes.

However, as you probably already know, we have no hope of cleaning ourselves up on our own — we can't make ourselves holy. That's what's so great about our holy God. He tells us to be holy, then works in us by the power of the Holy Spirit to change us from the inside out.

We'll talk about this more in our last two days together, but for today, think on this truth: Our God is holy, and He wants us to reflect His holiness in all we say and do.

<< ASK >>

As those set apart by God, we're supposed to look different from the world around us. How does this make you feel? Are you someone who likes standing out or would you rather fit in? Why?

What are some ways that you (as a follower of Jesus) can look different from the rest of the world? (I'll give you a couple examples to get you started. You can forgive a friend who wronged you instead of holding a grudge. You can keep your mouth shut when others are gossiping. You can smile and say hello to the kid that everyone else ignores. Okay — your turn!)

<< PRAY >>

Father God, I praise You today for being holy. Everything about You is perfect, pure, right, and good. Although I feel far from holy, I trust that You are doing a holy work in me. Please change me from the inside out, one baby step at a time.

<< LIVE >>

An appropriate response to learning about our holy God is worship. This week, incorporate listening to worship music into your daily routine. Try listening when you get dressed in the morning, in the car, and/or before you go to bed at night. Music is a great way to focus your heart and mind on the goodness and perfection of God.

#29 He is ...
PATIENT

(The LORD Who Sanctifies: Jehovah Mekadesh)

And I am certain that God, who began the good work within you, will continue his work until it is finally finished on the day when Christ Jesus returns. (Philippians 1:6)

Yesterday we learned that God is holy, and as His chosen children, He wants us to be holy too. No big deal, right? God just wants you and me to become perfectly pure in every way, without even a hint of sin. No problem, right?

Wrong! Not only is that impossible, but if we're being honest, that kind of life may not even sound appealing. So, before we talk about how we become holy, let's talk about what it's not.

First off, we don't become holy by going to church every time the doors are open. Holiness isn't about being more religious. It's also not about perfectly following all the rules. Holiness isn't about cleaning ourselves up on the outside — it's not about our behavior. Instead, holiness is something that we continually become as God changes us from the inside out through a process called *sanctification*. (He is The LORD Who Sanctifies.)

Sanctification is the ongoing work of God inside us that sets us apart from sin so we can be set apart for His purposes. Listen to the way Timothy, a young believer in the early church, puts it:

> The Lord wants to use you for special purposes, so make yourself clean from all evil. Then you will be holy, and the Master can use you. You will be ready for any good work. (2 Timothy 2:21 ERV)

Whether we realize it now or not, God wants to use us in specific ways to accomplish His amazing plans and purposes. In order to prepare us for that good work, He has to cut away the sin in our lives that holds us back and makes us ineffective for use.

Without our even realizing it, that process began the day we first put our faith in Jesus. On that day He made us holy on the inside — He put His Spirit in us and gave us hearts that can know and love Him (Ezekiel 36:26). Then, slowly and steadily, as long as we're willing, God continues to work in us, cutting away sin and purifying our lives so He can use us for His special purposes.

Although this process is unquestionably long (with many ups and downs), God is altogether patient with us. Picture Him like a parent teaching his child how to walk. Parents don't get mad or frustrated with their little ones for falling down. Instead, they cheer them on, constantly encouraging them and offering a hand of support with every new step they take. God is like that, too. He isn't mad at us for falling down (for messing up or making bad decisions). He simply wants us to reach out our hand when we fall down so He can pick us back up again. His desire for us is that we keep moving forward, one baby step at a time.

> The LORD is merciful and compassionate, slow to get angry and filled with unfailing love. (Psalm 145:8)

You can trust, today and always, that the God who began a good work in you won't give up on you mid-design. He will keep perfecting you until you see Him face-to-face.

<< ASK >>

Describe the process of sanctification in your own words.

What does it mean to you that God is patient with you as you learn, fall down, and grow?

<< PRAY >>

Heavenly Father, thank You for being so patient with me. You are merciful and compassionate, slow to get angry and filled with unfailing love. Teach me how to lean into my relationship with You as You make me holy from the inside out. I want to be useful and ready for every good work You have prepared in advance for me. Thank You for never giving up on me.

<< LIVE >>

The author of Hebrews compares our Christian life to running a race. Read the verses written for you below:

> We have all these great people around us as examples. Their lives tell us what faith means. So we, too, should run the race that is before us and never quit. We should remove from our lives anything that would slow us down and the sin that so often makes us fall. We must never stop looking to Jesus. He is the leader of our faith, and he is the one who makes our faith complete. He suffered death on a cross. But he accepted the shame of the cross as if it were nothing because of the joy he could see waiting for him. And now he is sitting at the right side of God's throne. (Hebrews 12:1–2 ERV)

If you picture your relationship with Jesus like a race, what in your life is slowing you down from an all-out sprint after all that He has for you? (For example, a lack of desire, comparing yourself to others, or guilt from past choices.)

What sins are tripping you up and making you fall along the way?

Talk to Jesus today about your desire to cut away the things that are slowing you down and tripping you up so that you can look more and more like Him every day.

#30 He is …
LIFE-CHANGING

(The LORD Who Sanctifies: Jehovah Mekadesh)

This means that anyone who belongs to Christ has become a new person. The old life is gone; a new life has begun!
(2 Corinthians 5:17)

Congratulations! You've officially made it to our final lesson together. I'm so proud of you for investing in your relationship with Jesus by seeking Him through this book. Although I'm well aware that not all learning is fun, I hope you've enjoyed learning about this great and mighty God we serve. I pray as we turn this last page together that you can say with confidence that God is *bigger* and *better* than you ever thought He was!

In our last lesson, we talked about how God never gives up on us mid-design. Throughout our whole lives, our patient and faithful God will keep working in us so that we can partner with Him to accomplish every good work that He's prepared in advance for us to do.

In case you haven't discovered this yet, I want you to know that following God is *not* boring. If you're feeling bored, there's a good chance you're focusing on the wrong things. Remember, Jesus didn't come to simply clean us up on the outside or to make us follow a bunch of rules. Following rules (although necessary) can be boring, but walking with Jesus isn't about perfectly following a long list of rules. Instead, He came to change our lives completely from the inside out. He came to make us brand new!

Did you know that once you place your faith in Jesus, God no longer sees the old you? To Him, your old life is dead and gone (including all your mistakes, failures, and bad choices). Now He only sees you through the perfect lens of Jesus. And in Jesus, all things are made new.

As you continue to grow in your relationship with Jesus and learn to walk with Him each day, He'll begin changing you from the inside out, one baby step at a time. He'll change the way you think by giving you new thoughts and new desires that are rooted in His truth. These new thoughts and desires will inspire new hopes, new dreams, a new perspective, and a new purpose.

Before you know it, Jesus, your faithful guide and friend, will invite you to step out of your comfort zone to do things with Him that you never thought you could do. He'll invite you to love like you've never loved before, trust like you've never trusted before, and live a life that's more fulfilling than your wildest dreams. Following Jesus will become the greatest adventure of your life.

Jesus is life-changing, and without a doubt, He's everything you'll ever need. Will you trust Him today?

<< ASK >>

Is following Jesus boring to you? Why or why not?

Do you believe that God is who He says He is? If not, what's holding you back from believing?

How has Jesus already changed your life?

<< PRAY >>

Father God, thank You for loving me, pursuing me, and staying with me no matter what. I don't know what my future holds, but I know You will always be with me, walking with me and changing me to become more like You. I want all that You have for me, Lord. Teach me every day how to know, follow, and trust You.

<< LIVE >>

Although God is the one who makes us holy, He asks that we participate in the process of sanctification. Our part in the process is to dedicate ourselves fully (heart, body, mind, strength, and soul) to the Lord. Before you close your book for the last time, write a prayer to God. Thank Him for what you've learned about Him, and tell Him you want to know Him more. There's always more of God to be found.

He is ...
HOLY,
PATIENT,
& LIFE-CHANGING.

Look back over Lessons 28–30. What stuck out to you? Did you learn something new? What is one truth you want to remember about God this week?

<< READ IT >>
- ☐ Isaiah 6:1–8
- ☐ John 17:13–19
- ☐ 1 Thessalonians 5:23–24

<< WRITE IT >>

Look up Romans 12:2. Write the verse in the space provided.

<< SHARE IT >>

Share with someone the one big truth you learned about God this week. Who are you going to tell? _____ (Now go do it!)

He is …

OUR SOURCE, CREATOR, SUSTAINER; OUR OWNER, IN CHARGE, PAYING ATTENTION; CONSTANT, PRESENT & ACTIVE, A PROMISE KEEPER; IN CONTROL, ALL-POWERFUL, GOOD; ALL-SUFFICIENT, SATISFYING, ENOUGH; OUR HELPER, GUIDE, PROTECTOR; PROVIDER, NEVER LATE, THE ANSWER; OUR HEALER, COMFORTER, REDEEMER; OUR DEFENDER, STRENGTH, VICTORY; HOLY, PATIENT, & LIFE-CHANGING.

CPSIA information can be obtained
at www.ICGtesting.com
Printed in the USA
LVHW051051020619
619867LV00040B/2287/P